Ancient Roman Women

Brian Williams

H **www.heinemann.co.uk/library**
Visit our website to find out more information about **Heinemann Library** books.

To order:
 Phone 44 (0) 1865 888066
 Send a fax to 44 (0) 1865 314091
💻 Visit the Heinemann Bookshop at www.heinemann.co.uk/library to browse our catalogue and order online.

First published in Great Britain by Heinemann Library, Halley Court, Jordan Hill, Oxford OX2 8EJ, part of Harcourt Education. Heinemann is a registered trademark of Harcourt Education Ltd.

Designed by Tinstar Design (www.tinstar.co.uk)
Illustrated by Jeff Edwards
Originated by Ambassador Litho Ltd
Printed by Wing King Tong in Hong Kong, China

ISBN 0 431 14562 8
06 05 04 03 02
10 9 8 7 6 5 4 3 2 1

British Library Cataloguing in Publication Data
Williams, Brian
      Ancient Roman women. – (People in the past)
      1. Women – Rome – History – Juvenile literature
      2. Civilization, Modern – Roman influences – Juvenile literature
      3. Rome – Social conditions – 510–30 B.C. – Juvenile literature
      I.Title
      305.4'0937

Acknowledgements
The Publishers would like to thank the following for permission to reproduce photographs:
AKG London pp7 (Gilles Mermet, Musee du Bardo), 9 (Erich Lessing, Musee du Louvre), 10 (Gilles Mermet, Museum of Tunisia), 12 (Vatican Museum), 14 (Erich Lessing, Museum Ostia), 18 (Erich Lessing, Musee du Louvre), 19 (Gilles Mermet, Museum of Tunisia), 26 (Erich Lessing, Kunsthistorisches Museum, Vienna), 28, 37 (Erich Lessing, National Museum of Archaeology, Naples), 39 (Vatican Museum); Ancient Art & Architecture Collection pp6, 17, 20, 23 (Piazza Armerina, Sicily), 24, 29, 36, 38, 41; British Museum p16; John Seely pp30, 42; Scala Art Resource pp11, 27, 32, 40; The Vindolanda Trust p34.

Cover photograph reproduced with permission of The Art Archive (Eileen Tweedy).

Every effort has been made to contact copyright holders of any material reproduced in this book. Any omissions will be rectified in subsequent printings if notice is given to the Publisher.

Contents

Words appearing in the text in bold, **like this**, are explained in the Glossary.

Roman men and women

◄▷ ◄▷ ◄▷ ◄▷ ◄▷ ◄▷ ◄▷ ◄▷ ◄▷ ◄▷ ◄▷ ◄▷ ◄▷ ◄▷ ◄▷ ◄

Who were the Romans? To us today, they are probably the most famous of all ancient peoples. The Romans believed their history began in 753 BC. That is 753 years before the birth of Jesus Christ. For almost 500 years they ruled one of the great **empires** of history.

The Romans lived in Italy. Their city of Rome was the centre of the Roman Empire and, for a time, the biggest city in the world. There are many reminders of Roman times, because wherever they conquered, the Romans built roads and towns. The best-preserved Roman town is Pompeii in Italy, buried by ash from the volcano Vesuvius in AD 79. Much more evidence is hidden, beneath fields and below the busy streets of modern cities.

The first Romans

The first Romans were farmers. They lived in **thatched** huts built on seven hills beside the River Tiber in a region called Latium in central

This map shows the Roman world in AD 100, when the empire was at its biggest. Most peoples in countries conquered by Rome copied Roman ways.

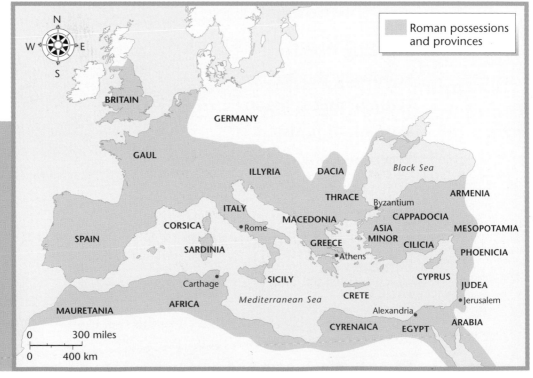

Italy. Roman mothers told their children the old story of how Rome had been founded by twin brothers named Romulus and Remus, who were raised by a wolf.

In about 510 BC the Romans set up a **republic**. Farmers and shepherds became **citizen**-soldiers, who conquered not just all Italy, but also many other lands. In 27 BC Rome became an empire, ruled by **emperors**. The emperors were men, though often powerful women helped to rule alongside them.

Roman society

Roman society was run by men. On a Roman farm, men and their sons did most of the work. Women ran the house, prepared meals, and did the important work of **spinning** and **weaving**. As Rome grew bigger, male and female slaves did more work. A few rich women enjoyed a life of luxury, but most women worked hard all their lives. Some helped their husbands. Other women, like the wives of Roman soldiers serving abroad, worked to support themselves and their children. In this book, you will discover more about the daily lives of Roman women, rich and poor.

The roles of women

In the Roman world, most women were less well educated than men, and in the Roman family, the father was more important than the mother. Even so 'womanhood' was important in Roman thinking. There were female gods and women priests. There were women artists and writers. Some Roman women had great power and influence, like the empress Agrippina. A few women, like Hypatia of Alexandria, became skilled in science. This book will tell you more about these powerful women and why they were respected, and sometimes feared.

Mothers and slaves

Roman men often idealized women – comparing them to **goddesses**, who were incredibly beautiful and powerful. Real women had a harder time. They had to work hard and raise children. For all women, bearing children was seen as their main job. Sentimental Romans thought of Rome itself as the 'Mother' of the nation. Most men thought a good woman should be strong and fearless (like a good man).

The Sabine women

One of Rome's favourite stories about women was told by the Greek writer Plutarch. According to legend, when Romulus founded the city of Rome, there were no women. Romulus asked neighbouring **tribes** to let the Roman men choose wives from their women. They refused. So the Romans kidnapped young women from the Sabine tribe. This led to war between the two peoples, until the Sabine women persuaded the men to make peace and live as one nation. This story shows how Romans liked to idealize women, especially the women who were the ancestors of all Romans.

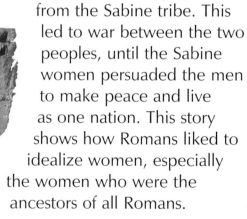

This stone carving shows a wet nurse called Severina, with the baby she was hired to feed and look after. A rich mother could pay a poor woman with a nursing baby, to breast-feed her baby as well. The carving comes from Severina's tombstone in Cologne, Germany.

Mothers without rights

Roman women were respected as mothers. Many women were never married at all; some through choice, others because their families were unable to offer enough money to attract a suitable husband.

Roman women had very few rights in law. A free woman was a little better off than a slave, but not much. She could not inherit all her husband's property after he died, nor could she leave all her money to her children. A wife could not divorce her husband, but he could divorce her.

Women as slaves

Rich women had the most personal freedom. Slave women had none. Many women in the Roman world were slaves, and most Romans thought this was perfectly natural. Slaves were sold in slave markets. A note hung around each slave's neck described any special skills they had. Young and attractive female slaves were sold for the highest prices.

Women slaves worked in homes, farms and workshops. In the home of a rich family, female slaves cleaned, cooked and served food. They also washed clothes, did their mistress's hair and helped her to dress. Her master might father a slave woman's children. A rich Roman might keep up to 100 slaves in his town house, while some nobles owned as many as 10,000 slaves, who worked on their country estates or **villas**.

A slave holds the mirror as her mistress does her hair, in this Roman mosaic.

Growing up

Roman women could not be heads of families. A family was headed by the father, the *pater familias* (**Latin** for 'father of the family'). He ruled everyone in his familia or household – wife, children, other relatives, servants and slaves. If a baby was unwanted or born weak, he could order it to be abandoned or left to die. A man could even order the death of his wife or children.

Babies

Most babies were warmly welcomed into the family, lifted up by the father as a sign that he accepted the child as his. A new baby was placed on the ground to cry for a while, before being washed and clothed. A baby girl was named when she was eight days old. In early Rome, girls had only their family name and one other, such as 'the Elder', 'the Younger', or simply a number! Later, a girl had two names, her family or **clan** name (such as Julia) and a form of her father's name (Augusta). Men usually had three names: forename (Gaius), clan name (Julius) and surname (Caesar).

At their naming ceremony, girls and boys were given a lucky charm. Babies were often reared by a nurse, often a slave or **freedwoman**. A woman who failed to have children could be divorced by her husband. Only a man could legally adopt a child.

Childhood and schooldays

Little girls did not have much time to spend in play, though popular toys (such as board games and wooden dolls) have been found by **archaeologists**. Slave children were often hard at work by the age of five, so never went to school. Lucky girls with rich parents were taught at home. Other girls went to school with their brothers, under the care of a nurse. Girls went to the elementary school (*ludus*), where they were taught to read and write. Only boys went on to the high school, or *grammaticus*, to study for careers in the law and government. Clever girls did any further studying at home.

Emperor's wild child

The **emperor** Augustus had one child – a daughter named Julia. He divorced her mother when Julia was only a baby, and she was brought up very strictly. She was married at sixteen, and again at eighteen. After her second husband died, she was forced to marry Tiberius, the son of her stepmother Livia. Neither partner was happy, and Julia began a series of love affairs. Her wild behaviour caused a scandal. Despite her popularity with the people, she was banished. After Tiberius became emperor, he cruelly allowed her to starve to death.

The Romans believed in family life. This relief carving from a 2nd-century tomb shows a mother feeding her baby, the father with a toddler and (right) a boy driving a miniature chariot.

Marriage

Under Roman law, girls could marry at the age of twelve. The usual age was around fourteen, but some women waited until their late teens or twenties. Parents arranged many marriages, and some brides were **betrothed** to their husbands while still babies. Roman husbands were quite often much older than their wives.

Wedding preparations

Before the wedding day, a girl said goodbye to her childhood toys and dolls. She 'gave them away' by dedicating them to the love-**goddess** Venus, or to household spirits called the *lares* and *penates*, which Romans believed watched over the family home. With the toys went the *bulla* or good luck charm worn by a girl since her naming ceremony.

The great day

Before dawn, a pig or sheep was **sacrificed** so that **omens** could be read from the animal's insides. The wedding took place at the bride's house, which was decorated with ribbons, flowers and wreaths made of myrtle and laurel. The bride's attendant, a married woman, joined the hands of the bride and her new husband. They were then married.

This picture of a Roman wedding shows the bride in her wedding dress (centre). Paintings show brides wearing white dresses, with orange veils on their heads. The wedding feast included wedding cake. The Romans thought June was the luckiest month for weddings.

Fathers or **guardians** signed the marriage contract. This set out the financial arrangements between the families (the bride's parents usually had to make gifts to the man and his family). People prayed to the goddess Juno, asking her to watch over the couple and a sacrifice was offered to Jupiter, king of the gods. Everyone wished the pair good luck, and the wedding feast began.

Engagement rings

Just like many couples today, Romans gave rings as a sign of love. Before the wedding, the man gave the woman a ring, which she wore on the third finger of her left hand. Romans believed that a nerve ran from this finger straight to the heart. People today still wear engagement or wedding rings on the same 'ring finger'.

The feast lasted almost all day. When the bridal pair made ready to leave, the man pretended to tear the unwilling bride away from her mother. This game reminded everyone of the legend telling how Roman men had made off with the Sabine women. Then the bridal procession left for the new husband's home. Two boys held the bride's hands while another carried a torch before her. Passers-by joined the procession, singing wedding songs. Children scrambled to catch coins and nuts tossed by the husband to the crowd. These gifts were thrown to bring luck and as a sign of his generosity.

A new home

At her new home, the bride wound wool round the doorposts, smeared them with fat and hung them with garlands. This was done to bring good luck into her new home. After carrying her inside, her husband offered her fire and water to show she was now mistress of the house. She was placed on a bed, and the guests left. Next day, the husband gave his wife presents and they threw a party. The bridal bed took pride of place in the *atrium*, or main hall, of the house. It became yet another good luck charm. Roman couples often left the bridal couch in the *atrium* as a symbol and souvenir of the marriage, although they slept in a separate bedroom.

Silent partners

What we know about the Romans – from pictures, writings, **inscriptions** on tombstones – often tells us more about men than about women. Women were often 'silent partners', looking after the home and children. Although official records seldom mention women, many women must have helped to run family estates, businesses, shops and farms. Women whose husbands were away from home on business saw to it that family life went on smoothly.

Separate lives, different rules

We can get a good idea of what a Roman house was like from the remains of buildings preserved at the towns of Pompeii and Herculaneum under ash and mud from the volcano Vesuvius in AD 79. In the town house of a wealthy family, there was a central room called an *atrium*, open to the sky. Men and women dined together in the *triclinium*, or dining room. Pictures show women sitting on chairs, while men lie on couches.

A stone memorial to Marcus Porcius Cato, known as Cato the Censor, with his wife. This Roman lawyer and writer had strict views on how husbands and wives should behave.

Women had their own bedrooms, which they shared with small children. A wealthy woman often saw little of her husband during the day, when he was working in town or running his business. Only in the evening might husband and wife enjoy time together. Among slaves, poor farmers and city workers, partnerships were less formal and more easy-going. Poor people's homes were smaller, so couples spent more time together, and with their children.

A Roman wife was supposed to be loyal to her husband. If he had girlfriends, she was expected to 'forgive and forget'. Private lives were supposed to be very private. The Romans disliked public displays of emotion, and high-ranking men rarely showed affection to their wives outside the home. A politician named Manilius, who hoped to be elected **consul**, was expelled from the **Senate**. His 'crime', according to the lawyer Cato, was to kiss his wife in front of their daughter! Again, poorer Romans were probably a lot less stuffy.

Problems for a young wife

A young wife often had a difficult time at first. As a newcomer in her husband's family, she had to follow the advice of her mother-in-law (her husband's mother), who had the final say in most things. Having children gave a wife new importance, particularly if she had sons. Mother-in-law remained the senior woman in the family, until she died. Then the wife took over her position within the family.

Fulvia – a wife who stayed loyal

Fulvia, wife of the Roman general Mark Antony, is an example of a loyal Roman wife. She was first married in 58 BC, before she was 17. Her husband Clodius, a politician, was murdered, leaving her with two children. She helped bring his killer to justice. Her second husband Curio, a friend of Clodius, left her with a young son to go off to Africa. Her third husband was Mark Antony, who wanted to rule the Roman world. Fulvia bore Antony two sons, and helped his political career. She got little thanks because he went to Egypt, where he fell in love with Egypt's queen Cleopatra. Poor Fulvia died in Sicily, after falling ill on her way home to Rome from Greece. She was between 30 and 35 years old.

When a marriage ended

Divorce was common in ancient Rome, particularly among wealthy families. A common cause was the wife's 'failure' to bear a son. Some men also looked for a new wife to further their ambitions in politics or the army. Other marriages simply broke down, and the partners split up.

A husband could divorce his wife, but a woman could not divorce a man. A woman who had no children could be divorced. If she fell in love with another man, it was her husband's duty to divorce her, or he might lose his claim to her dowry, the property given by his wife's family at the time of the marriage.

Death and funerals

Death ended many partnerships. Many Roman women died before their husbands, at what would be a young age today (in their thirties). They often died as a result of illnesses after having children, or because a pregnancy went seriously wrong.

Tomb carvings show Roman families mourning a dead relative. Here the sword, helmet and shield show that the dead man was a soldier.

Caesar's wife

Julius Caesar divorced his wife Pompeia after a scandal that seems odd to us today. A man named Clodius disguised himself as a woman to get into an all-women religious meeting, at which Pompeia was present. There was no evidence of any wrongdoing, but Caesar ended the marriage. He is reported to have said, pompously, that 'Caesar's wife must be above suspicion'.

Roman funerals

Before a funeral the women of a household helped prepare the body for burial, assisted by professional **undertakers** and slaves. They also prepared a feast for the family and funeral guests. Funerals were usually held at night. The funeral procession moved slowly to the cemetery outside the city, accompanied by musicians, torch-bearers and singers who sang the praises of the dead person. Women wore their hair loose, as a sign of mourning. A wife would stay in mourning for a dead husband for almost a year. She would not go to parties or meals with friends, and wore no jewellery.

Cremation (burning a dead body) was the usual form of funeral in Rome before AD 100. Later, and especially after most Romans became Christians, burial was the rule. Women were buried with personal possessions such as jewels or favourite oil lamps. Husbands paid for their wives' funerals. Unmarried women put aside money to make sure they got a 'respectable' final send-off.

Marrying again

A **widow** could remarry, and many did. A woman had no right to the family home after her husband was dead, unless he had said so in his **will**. For a soldier's wife, sudden death brought practical problems as well as sorrow. She had no help from the government. An officer's wife knew her army house would pass to her husband's replacement, while she was left to build a new life as best she could.

A well-ordered home

Roman parents took their responsibilities seriously. The **historian** Tacitus did not think much of parents who allowed slaves to look after children. He wrote that slaves filled children's heads with 'stories and lies', so that all the children talked about were actors and gladiators!

Young women were naturally nervous about having babies. Pregnancy could be dangerous and many women died in childbirth. Some Romans had big families, but because so many babies died, three or four children made up a more usual family.

Left in charge

Until the children went to school, their mother did most of the 'parenting'. She ran the home, saw to it that the children were clean and fed, and made sure that slaves did their work properly. She kept the house keys, as a sign that she was in charge of the household.

A man usually left the house early, finished work by noon and had a doze after lunch. He then spent the afternoon relaxing at the baths, or perhaps watching gladiators fight. He expected to return to a well-ordered home, and his dinner. The mistress of a wealthy household might go out to the shops herself. More often she sent a slave to the market to buy fresh meat, bread and vegetables.

A pottery cup with a spout, used for feeding babies and also sick adults. It was found at South Shields in north-east England.

Stay at home and spin

The **emperor** Augustus insisted that his daughter Julia should spin and weave. His wife Livia is said to have made his warm winter underwear herself. Augustus wanted to show the Romans that no woman, not even an emperor's daughter, should be too proud to do these traditional household tasks. Julia, who was high-spirited and intelligent, thought she and her rich friends had better things to do!

Of course, very few women had a comfortable home and a rich husband. Many poor women set up home with equally poor men. Such couples raised families in a room in an apartment block, or in a country cottage so run-down that no one else wanted it. Only rich women enjoyed home comforts, and had any leisure time.

Spinning time

One of the most important jobs done by women was making clothes for the family. On the way to her new home, a Roman bride carried **spinning** tools – a **distaff** and **spindle**. This was an old custom. Most Roman women knew how to spin thread and weave it into cloth. Tufts of raw wool or **linen** fibres were held on the distaff, a wooden stick. The mass of fibres was then pulled and twisted together into a thread and wound onto another stick called the spindle. Some big houses had workshops where female slaves did the spinning and **weaving**, under the eye of their mistress.

A Roman woman spinning with a spindle, which twisted the wool threads as it spun. She holds the distaff in her left hand.

Household chores

Cleaning the house took up much of a Roman woman's time. There was no electricity to power machines for washing, drying or ironing clothes, or cleaning rugs. Slaves were the only labour-saving aids available!

Sweeping and polishing

Stone-paved or tiled floors needed sweeping and scrubbing to get rid of the dust people brought in from the street or the farm. Roman brushes were made from wood with bristles of animal hair or plant fibres. Twig brooms were cheap and useful outside.

Women probably used dusters, though it is impossible to prove that a scrap of cloth found by **archaeologists** on a **site** was actually a duster. The house-proud Roman woman scurried round with feather dusters and dustpan, just as some people do today. Most furniture was made of wood, and polished with oil and beeswax.

Lighting and heating

Nightfall brought darkness, inside and outside the home. Women lit candles and looked after oil lamps, filling the lamps with olive oil and trimming the wicks. A tablespoon of oil burned for two hours, but a single lamp did not give much light. The Romans also burned cheap rush lights, made from reeds dipped in wax or animal fat.

Roman clothes, such as a woman's stola, or **tunic**, and a man's **toga**, were made from long lengths of cloth (shown here). They were awkward to wash and heavy when wet. Drying and washing must have been difficult in colder, wetter parts of the Roman **Empire**.

In winter, or on cool nights in summer, wood-burning braziers (metal baskets) kept rooms warm. Fetching wood or **charcoal**, and cleaning out the fire, was a job for a slave.

Some houses had piped water, but most people had to fetch water for drinking, cooking and washing. Women carried buckets to the nearest well or public tank.

Very little Roman furniture has survived the centuries, so we have to look at pictures to see what it was like. This mosaic from a house near Pompeii shows a woman relaxing on a long couch.

Washing

This was a weekly chore for Roman women, and was done

Mistress of the hypocaust

The biggest and best Roman houses had underfloor warm air central heating. The hypocaust, as it is known, provided warmth and heated water too. The mistress of a big **villa** made sure the heating and hot water system was working, especially when visitors were being entertained.

by hand. Big tubs were set up outside in the courtyard for the family wash, but small everyday items could be washed in a bowl in the kitchen. Blankets or other large items might be taken to a nearby stream, and pounded against stones to bash out the dirt. Clothes were washed in cold water, using a kind of soap called lye, which was made from goat fat and wood ash. This smelt bad and made your hands sore.

Wet washing was spread over bushes or on the ground to dry in the sun and wind. Clothes were ironed with a round stone or smooth lump of glass, or pressed in a clothes press. Rich families sent their dirty washing to a professional laundry – in most towns, there were 'wash-shops', where women did most of the work.

In the kitchen

Women made sure that the family was fed. Even where slaves did the cooking, the woman of the house ordered the shopping from the local market.

The cooks at work

The Roman cooker was a stone table on which lay glowing embers of **charcoal**. Food was cooked in pots, pans and basins set on iron **tripods** above the hot charcoal. Women also had beehive-shaped ovens made of bricks and tiles, heated by a fire of charcoal or wood. When it was hot, the ashes were raked out, and the food – bread, meat or pastry – was put into the oven.

Women's work in the kitchen could be hard. Flour was made by grinding grain between two heavy stones. Kitchen tools similar to those of today included knives, ladles, spoons, strainers, choppers, and **pestles and mortars** for crushing herbs or nuts. Cooks used frying pans and baking trays. For soups and stews they hung large metal pots from chains over the fire.

This mosaic from the 2nd to 4th century AD shows some of the foods Romans liked to eat. Only rich people feasted on such a range of dishes, which included gazelle, fowl, vegetables and fruit.

Cutlery and washing up

Women took great care of kitchen equipment. Iron knives were valuable; so most families used cheaper bronze knives. Spoons were made of metal, horn or bronze. The Romans did not use forks, and often ate with their fingers. Glass was easily broken and expensive, so olive oil and wine were kept in large pottery jars called *amphorae*. In a grand house, food was served on a big round dish called a *discus*, and on smaller plates of silver, bronze and **pewter**. Most ordinary people ate off wood or pottery dishes. Women washed up in bowls, using water but no washing-up liquid! They cleaned metal dishes by rubbing them with sand.

> ### Promise not to tell anyone ...
> At a dinner party, a Roman lady would hang a rose above the table. This was a sign to her guests that anything said that evening should never be repeated. In an old story, Cupid had given a rose to the god of silence Harpocrates, to make sure no gossip was spread about his mistress, the love-**goddess** Venus.

Feeding the family

Women were expected to provide food for the family. Roman food was not much like Italian food today – no pasta, for one thing. Poor families made do with coarse bread, eaten with pea or bean soup, and porridge made from wheatmeal. Most Roman women were expert in housekeeping – in their homes, little was wasted.

Although Roman farmers were mostly men, women in the countryside and in town gardens grew vegetables and fruit. This produce helped to feed the family. While many Roman women must have been happy to cook a roast chicken or stewed hare for dinner once a month, rich Romans feasted on delicacies ranging from stuffed dormice to a whole roast pig! Women with time on their hands might browse through the recipes of the most famous Roman cookery writer, a man named Apicius, to decide what to give their guests at the next party.

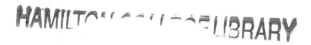

The life of a Roman lady

Rich women, with no household chores and with maids to wait on them, could enjoy a life of leisure. They shopped, lunched with friends, planned their gardens, went to the chariot races or watched the gladiators fighting in the arena. However, not all rich Roman women did nothing but play. Some, like the noblewoman Cornelia, were interested in learning and politics, or devoted themselves to their children.

Passing the time

In the big city of Rome, rich women could join in the smart social round, if they wished. Life in small towns was quieter. In the **provinces** the governor's wife often became the leader of local society, playing hostess to the wives of officials and army officers.

At home, with friends or children, women played guessing games (such as 'odd or even', with small stones), and a game like noughts and crosses. The poet Ovid thought every woman ought to be good at board games played with dice and counters. Play boards were made of pottery and wood, but there were also expensive marble boards that may have belonged to wealthy women.

The lady Cornelia

Rich women with brains were formidable **citizens**. Cornelia came from one of Rome's great noble families. Her father was the general Scipio Africanus, a hero of Rome. Cornelia had twelve children, whom she taught to think for themselves. Her two most talented sons, Tiberius and Gaius, known to history as the Gracchi, became reforming politicians. Cornelia called her sons 'her finest ornaments'. The Gracchi made many enemies. One was murdered; the other killed himself while under attack. After this tragedy, Cornelia retired to live near Naples. Her learning entertained all that met her, and Romans thought her the perfect 'Roman lady'.

Sports, hobbies and pets

The Romans were less keen on sport than the ancient Greeks, but it seems some women enjoyed outdoor games. A **mosaic** from Sicily shows two women wearing what look like bikinis and playing a ball game. Noblewomen may have gone hunting, though there is not much evidence for this. Gardening was a relaxation that many wealthy Roman women must have enjoyed, since gardens were a feature of most elegant homes.

We know that dogs or cats were kept as pets because the bones of these animals are often found near houses. Some were guard dogs or rat-catchers, but some must have been family pets. At Stanwick **villa** in Northamptonshire, England, the bones of a small dog were found in a Roman grave. Birds too were favourite pets.

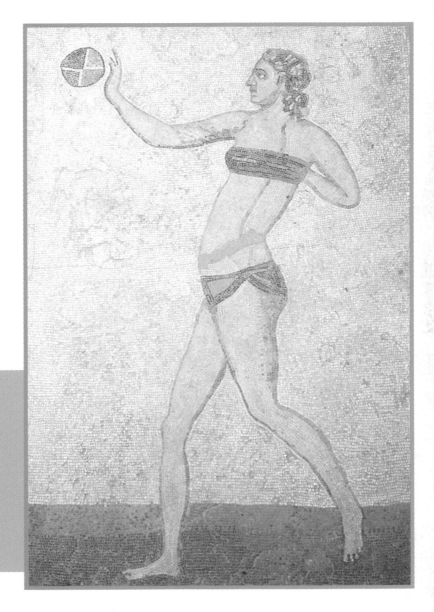

This mosaic shows a Roman woman playing a ball game. She may be playing a team game, similar to basketball or volleyball, but more likely she is simply enjoying a keep-fit routine.

What women wore

Women made clothes for their families, and tombstones show them holding spindles, **weaving** combs or balls of wool.

Top dressing

Roman women wore simple, loose clothes, much like those of the ancient Greeks. A long **tunic**, called a *stola*, was a robe with short sleeves or none at all. It could be tied round the waist. A brooch at the shoulder fastened the stola. Over it, a woman wore a long rectangle of cloth called the *palla*. This could be draped across the shoulders like a shawl, pulled up over the head like a cloak, or folded and wound as a scarf around the shoulders and neck. In cold weather, the palla could also double as a blanket. Some women wore a veil over their head and shoulders.

Most clothes were made of wool or **linen**. Wealthy women also wore silk imported from India or China, and liked bright colours, as can be seen from wall paintings. Poorer women made do with coarse brown or grey cloth, fastened with a treasured brooch or pin.

This 2nd-century **relief** sculpture of a wedding ceremony shows the bride wearing a full-length dress and veil. The man wears a toga, draped over his shoulder.

Underwear

Women wore a light linen tunic, like a petticoat, which in many statues is shown hanging below the *stola*. Underneath, they might wear a short, shirt-like *camisia*. A band of cloth, wound tight like a corset, was called the *strophium*. Women probably also wore linen briefs. It is likely that they slept in their underwear, as men seem to have done.

Cold weather clothes and shoes

In cold weather, women wore capes, shawls and scarves. They also wore woollen socks and stockings, and probably mittens. British women wore the Gallic coat, a wide loose tunic with sleeves. In colder parts of the **empire** like Britain, wool was more common than linen. Cotton, which came from Sudan and India, was very rare.

Women usually wore leather sandals or shoes, with wooden or, more often, leather soles. At home, they put on elegant slippers, some with wooden or cork soles to protect feet from hot, wet floors in the bathhouse. Women who could not afford shoes went barefoot.

The Roman wedding dress

Romans thought it was lucky for a bride to sleep in her white wedding dress the night before the wedding. In the morning her mother helped to tie a woollen waistband, fastened with a knot that only her new husband could untie. The bride's hair, parted into six ringlets by a spear-shaped curling iron, was tied with ribbons. She wore an orange veil, the *flammeum*, which hid her face, and a crown of flowers. She also wore yellow shoes – another good-luck charm to help her have children, and so succeed as a Roman wife.

High fashion

Ladies of the **emperor's** family set the fashion in Rome. Women in other cities copied Roman styles, though fashions did not change very much from one century to the next. While their clothes were mostly simple in style, rich women could show off by wearing jewels.

Roman jewellery

Romans loved gold, and Rome was a centre for goldsmiths' shops. Even some household furniture was made from gold and silver, as shown by objects found in Pompeii. As Rome's empire grew richer, ordinary people could afford gold rings, and rich people wore rings that were truly massive. Some rings bore their owner's name.

Women also wore bracelets, arm bands, headdresses and earrings (for pierced ears only). Romans liked colourful gems, such as topaz, emerald, rubies and sapphires, as well as pearls. Gold was worked into plaited wire bands and chains, and often set with gemstones. Women also wore **cameo** necklaces, or a pendant of gold coins bearing the emperor's picture. Poorer women wore jewellery made from a cheaper metal, such as bronze, set with coloured glass beads instead of precious stones.

Perfumes

Rich women wore perfumes, which were kept both at home and at the public baths. It was stored in jars and small glass bottles called *unguentaria*.

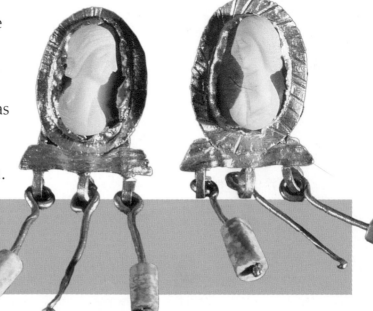

A pair of Roman cameo earrings, with a woman's profile set in gold. Most Roman gold came from Spain.

Bathing in milk

Vain Roman women with money would do almost anything to make themselves appear more attractive. When bathing in asses' milk became fashionable (Queen Cleopatra of Egypt did it), the Roman empress Poppaea travelled with a small herd of asses (donkeys), to supply her bathtime milk. This empress had two husbands before Nero, a cruel man who brought about her death in AD 65 by kicking her during a violent argument.

Frankincense, myrrh, balsam and cedar oil were used to make pleasant fragrances. Roman women also rubbed their bodies with scented oils, like the oils used for aromatherapy today. Poppaca Sabina, wife of the emperor Nero, liked a particularly strong perfume that was named after her.

Good hair days

Blonde hair, once thought 'common', became fashionable during the Roman **Empire** (after 27 BC). Many women bleached their hair or wore a blonde wig. **Henna** was used to dye hair dark red, a shade also thought desirable. Celtic women were admired for their natural red-brown hair. Dark hair for wigs was imported from as far away as India and long blonde hair from German prisoners was also much in demand.

A high society lady checked her looks in the small mirror of her make-up box. There were glass mirrors, but metal ones were cheaper and unbreakable. While she dressed, a servant would have held a large decorated mirror.

This bronze mirror dates from the 3rd century BC. The largest Roman mirrors had decorated handles for a servant to hold.

Hair and make-up

Although some male writers said no Roman woman should fuss about how she looked, many women in Rome used make-up, as women in ancient Greece and Egypt had done before them. The Roman writer Ovid wrote about cosmetics in a poem called *On Painting the Face*. To improve the skin, he advised using oyster shells mixed with water. For a face pack, why not try ten eggs and twelve narcissus (daffodil) bulbs, ground to a paste with honey, gum and skinned barley? Another poet, Horace, suggested a face pack made from crocodile dung!

Creams and cosmetics

What went into cosmetics was often a curious mixture. A popular skin cream was made from sweat and dirt taken from sheep's wool. Rouge, or blusher, to redden cheeks and lips was made from red **ochre** or the dregs (solid waste) of red wine. Face powder was used to cover up blemishes, such as spots or scars. Ovid's recommended face powder contained lupin seeds and white lead. Lead was poisonous, but gave a fashionable 'white' look. Chalk and dried berries were also used in face powders.

A make-up kit, found in Rome. It includes a mirror, comb, hairpins, a ring and a make-up pot.

Women liked their eyes to look good. The science writer Pliny wrote down a recipe for mascara that used bear's fat, and also mentions ants' eggs and squashed flies! Ash from fires was recommended for eye shadow, and soot or **charcoal** for outlining eyebrows.

Creams and ointments were kept in small pots, and powder in make-up flasks. Poorer women probably made their own cosmetics, imitating the looks of rich women they saw in the city. Ash and soot were not hard to come by.

Hair styles

Statues and paintings show various Roman hairstyles. Roman women usually wore their long hair parted in the middle and rolled up at the back of the head in a bun or topknot. A head of reddish-brown hair, found in a cemetery at Eboracum (York), was wound into a bun held in place by long pins. Hairpins were made of silver, or cheaper metals such as bronze and bone. Brushes and combs were made of wood, bone, antler or ivory.

Putting on the style

Rich women had the most elaborate hairstyles, with waves and curls. To curl straight hair, women used curling tongs. They wore hairnets made of gold or silver, decorated with precious stones. The most wealthy put on gold or silver **tiaras** for glittering parties.

A mosaic from Pompeii shows the hairstyle of a rich Roman woman. This elegant lady probably chose her best earrings and necklaces for the artist to paint her.

Health

Health care in the Roman world was a patchwork of traditional cures, superstition, and (if you could afford him) the local doctor. Doctors were always men. Although barred from medicine as a career, many women were healers, making traditional cures from herbs. Within the family, women acted as midwives and nurses.

Gods and shrines

When they were sick, the Romans turned to their gods for help. They would make an offering in a temple, or visit a **shrine** that was a centre of healing. Such healing centres were often located at spas or natural springs, or at other special places connected to a healing god. Sick people would come to drink and bathe in the spring's waters, and to pray in the god's shrine. A woman with a particular health problem might leave a small model of the affected body-part at the shrine. At Wroxeter, in England, **archaeologists** have found 35 plaster eyes at a health-shrine, showing that people with eye-trouble visited it.

The *apodyterium* or changing room of the women's baths at Herculaneum, in Italy. On the floor are **mosaic** pictures of sea creatures. Shelves were provided for bathers' clothes.

Weeds for worms

The Romans used plants to make medicines. For example, ground elder (now a troublesome garden weed) was used to treat gout. The herb meadowsweet was mixed with pig fat to make an ointment for rubbing on bumps, lumps and sore patches. Women passed on the remedies used by their mothers, such as powdered walnuts mixed with honey for earache, or crushed mint dropped 'into ears that have worms inside them'!

Child bearing

Without reliable methods of birth control (there was no contraceptive pill in Roman times), many women bore more children than was good for their health. Problems in pregnancy, such as a **miscarriage**, could be fatal. Many women died in childbirth or from infections afterwards, and a great many children died as babies. Yet for a married woman, to be childless could be a personal tragedy. Her husband could divorce her.

The baths

Women and men went to the public baths, not just to keep clean, but also to meet friends and relax. Children and slaves bathed for free, others paid a small charge. Men and women usually bathed separately, though mixed bathing did go on, much to the concern of town officials who tried to stop it. Most women bathers used the baths at 'women-only' times. A woman might bathe naked or in a two-piece swimsuit, or choose a large and more modest slip.

In **garrison** towns, army baths were open to local women as well as soldiers. In the hot steam-rooms, women sewed while they sweated and gossiped – lost sewing needles have been found. After sweating, bathers scraped away the dirt with a curved metal blade called a *strigil*. A hot bath was followed by a cold plunge, and they went home, refreshed.

Working women

Many Roman women worked, on country farms and **villas**, or in towns. Working women had a hard time, doing physical tasks and running a home as well.

The Romans did not have weekends or public holidays, but there were more than 30 religious festivals through the year. On these special days there was time for many women to relax, though probably not for slaves.

Many women worked in shops and markets. This relief carving shows a busy food shop, and the couple serving behind the counter are probably the shop's owners. The shop is a poulterers (selling poultry).

The writing on the wall

Walls of houses in Pompeii are covered with graffiti. Romans were always scrawling messages, often rude, on walls. Scribbles by men include comments on the best-looking women in town. Graffiti possibly written by women praise the latest star gladiator.

Women in business

Many working women were slaves, while free women helped run small businesses, such as shops, laundries and food stalls. Some **widows** took over the management of businesses from dead husbands. One of the leading women of Pompeii was Eumachia, a rich cloth-maker who built the cloth-makers' hall in the Forum. Her business friends paid for a statue in her honour. She was buried in one of the finest tombs in the Street of the Tombs, where important **citizens** of Pompeii were laid to rest.

Country women

Roman life was based on the land, and on the growing of food. Farm work, such as ploughing, sowing and harvesting was done almost entirely by men. However, women did their part to make sure country estates or villas ran smoothly. A villa was managed by an overseer, whose wife was in charge of the female workers, who washed wool, made cheese and prepared pickles.

Entertainers

Towns were centres of entertainment. Women entertainers were not thought respectable, but they seem to have been plentiful. In Pompeii, women ran taverns (inns) and served drinks in bars. Evidence from pictures, and from a burial in London, suggests that there were female gladiators. There were certainly women dancers and acrobats. They entertained in the houses of rich Romans, or travelled the country, performing at markets and festivals.

Following the legions

Men ran the Roman army. According to Roman law, only senior army officers were supposed to marry. When a general or **governor** led his troops off to fight in a far-off land, his wife went too, along with their children and slaves. From time to time, Roman **senators** complained that military wives were a nuisance, turning a **legion's** orderly march into 'an Eastern procession', plotting to get jobs for their relatives, and sending **centurions** dashing about the camp on silly errands.

Such criticisms were hard on women who were doing their duty. Wives of army officers shared the hardships, and dangers, of life on the **frontier**. They looked forward to letters from friends. We can read the writing tablet sent by Claudia Severa to her friend Sulpicia Lepidina, inviting her to her birthday party. Both women were married to army officers serving in north Britain, just before the Romans built Hadrian's Wall in AD 122–128.

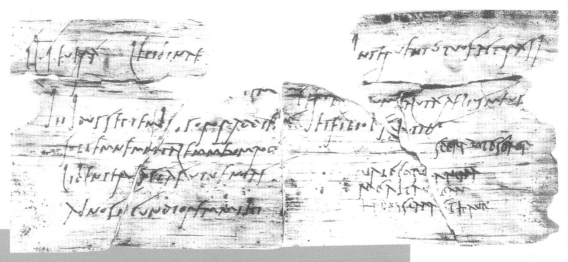

This is a fragment of a letter written by Claudia Severa to Sulpicia Lepidina, who lived with her husband at the Roman army fort at Vindolanda in Northumberland, England in about AD 100. Three letters survive, to tell us of the friendship between these two women on the frontier of the Roman **Empire**. One is a birthday invitation written by a scribe, but with a PS in Claudia Severa's own handwriting.

Women travellers

Roman army wives were among the first tourists. Sightseers could buy guidebooks and maps, to show places of interest such as the pyramids of Egypt, or the Oracle at Delphi in Greece. For ordinary travellers, roads could be dangerous. Travelling with the legions meant women felt safe from attack by bandits. Sea journeys could be even more dangerous, because of pirates and storms. Few Romans dared make a sea voyage in winter, for fear of shipwreck.

Following the legions

The backbone of the Roman army was the legion. An ordinary soldier in a legion looked forward to a gift of land when he retired after 25 years' service. He could then marry and settle down as a farmer. Until AD 197 a serving soldier was not supposed to marry, though many men did. Then the law was changed.

If a soldier was sent to a foreign land, his wife and children had to manage as best they could at home, or follow him. Centurions were often moved from one legion to another. We know of one centurion whose wife had a baby in York, England, before he was transferred to Arabia. Did she go too?

Tombstone evidence

Tombstones record the deaths of some army women and children. Memorials at Eboracum (York) in England, where there was a Roman army base, record the deaths of Corellia Optata aged 13, and of Julia Velva at 50. An army wife, Julia Secunda, reached what for a Roman was a good age. The widow of a soldier in the 20th Legion, she died at Caerleon in Wales, aged 75.

Women and religion

The Romans had many gods, whom they honoured with temples and statues. Jupiter was king of Rome's gods, but almost as important was his queen, Juno. She was **goddess** of light, and also watched over marriage, childbirth and newborn babies.

Goddesses of Rome

Female gods, or goddesses, were concerned mainly with love, marriage, children, and farming. Venus was the goddess of love, Ceres was a corn-goddess, Felicitas goddess of good luck, Tellus Mater the goddess of fruitfulness, Flora the goddess of flowers and Pomona looked after fruit trees. Minerva was a stern warrior, often shown in statues with an owl (symbol of wisdom) and a spear. She protected trade, learning and the arts, and was the Roman version of the powerful Greek goddess Athene.

The Vestals

Priests in Rome were almost all men, but one group of women were important. They were the Vestals. There were six of them, chosen as young as seven years old to serve in the temple of the goddess Vesta. Their duty was to look after her sacred 'hearth-fire'. Keeping the family fire alight may once have been the job of a younger daughter, while the men were busy outdoors, and mother and older sisters were **spinning** or **weaving**.

A statue of a Vestal. A Vestal stayed a Vestal for 30 years, and was forbidden to marry or have anything to do with men. To disobey this rule meant an awful punishment – being buried alive.

Foreign religions

Romans were fascinated by foreign religions. Aulus Plautius, who led the Roman army that invaded Britain in AD 43, took with him his wife Pomponia Graecina. She was later criticised for taking up a 'foreign religion', probably one she had come across in Britain. In Rome, some women became interested in 'mystery' religions, worshipping an Eastern 'Great Mother of the Gods'. Men often falsely accused the women who met together in secret religious 'clubs' of scandalous goings-on.

Vestals were treated with great respect, and guarded whenever they went out. They sat in special seats in the theatre. The house the Vestals lived in was so safe that rich people used it for storing their **wills**.

Religion at home

At home, the father led the family in religious **rituals**. Most homes had a **shrine**, a special place with an **altar** where gifts were made to the gods. The Romans generally allowed people to worship whatever gods they liked. If a woman chose, she could worship different gods from those of her husband.

From the 1st century AD, Christianity had a strong appeal to many women in the Roman world. It offered a hopeful view of an afterlife, and was more open to poor women (it did not call for rich gifts to the temple god). Christian teachings outlawed some old Roman practices, such as the killing of unwanted babies. Early Christian writers were rather stern, and told women to put away their make-up and wear plain clothes.

This Roman wall painting from the 1st–3rd century AD, shows a woman making a sacrifice, or offering to a god.

Women of power

There were no female **emperors**. However, the most influential Roman women controlled men in power, usually behind the scenes but at times openly. Wives of emperors schemed for their sons and grandsons, and a few did not shrink from murder.

Women to fear

Messalina, the third wife of the emperor Claudius, was certainly feared. She tried to control her husband, while carrying on scandalous affairs with his officials. She even persuaded Claudius to execute a **senator** who refused to do what she wished. She was finally unmasked by a secretary, who told Claudius that Messalina had secretly married another man while he was away, and was plotting to overthrow him. Claudius had her put to death in AD 48.

Claudius then made another mistake, by marrying his niece Agrippina, who was equally power-mad. She persuaded Claudius to adopt her son Nero, so that Nero should be the next emperor, not Claudius's own son. In AD 54 Claudius died from a mysterious illness. Did Agrippina poison him, with mushrooms? Most Romans thought she had; though not all modern **historians** think so.

After Nero became emperor, Agrippina (now known as 'empress') tried to tell him what to do. Nero did not care for this, especially when his mother began interfering in his love life. He first tried to drown her, in a boat with holes in it, but she swam ashore. Finally he had Agrippina murdered in her **villa**.

Agrippina, wife of Emperor Claudius, is often called 'the Younger' to distinguish her from her mother, who had the same name.

Agrippina, villain or victim?

Empress Agrippina, the 'poison-empress', was born in AD 15. Her mother starved to death, possibly on the orders of her grandfather, Emperor Tiberius. Her brother was the mad emperor Caligula (murdered in AD 41). First exiled for plotting against her brother, she was later accused of poisoning her second husband. She married Emperor Claudius in AD 49, but was blamed for his death five years later. No surprise then that Agrippina too died a violent death, murdered by her son's command.

Power play and murder

Power politics were complex and often dangerous. Syrian-born Julia Domna was the powerful wife of a later emperor, Septimus Severus, who ruled from AD 193 to AD 211. She was a clever woman. Her two sons, Caracalla and Geta, became joint rulers of Rome. They loathed one another so much that Caracalla murdered Geta. Caracalla became sole emperor, and while he was away with the army, Julia ran things in Rome.

When an army officer murdered Caracalla in AD 217, Julia Domna starved herself to death. Her sister, Julia Maesa, wife of a Roman senator, used her influence to win over the army and overthrow the new emperor Macrinus, who had schemed Caracalla's murder. She persuaded the **legions** in Syria (her homeland) to make her grandson Elagabalus emperor. When he turned out to be weak and corrupt, she turned to her daughter Julia Mamaea's teenage son, Alexander. Elagabalus was murdered and Alexander became emperor. Grandmother Julia Maesa held power until her death in AD 226, after which Julia Mamaea then tried to interfere in the government. Enemies murdered Emperor Alexander and his interfering mother in AD 235. Perhaps a quiet home life wasn't so bad after all!

A marble bust of Julia Domna. Born in Syria, she was the daughter of a high **priest**, and had many friends among Rome's writers and artists. While visiting Britain with Emperor Severus, she questioned British prisoners about their customs and beliefs.

Women's place in Roman life

Roman men preferred women to keep out of public life. The Roman **law codes** tell us how men expected women to behave. If a woman broke the law, she could expect punishment but she had no say in making those laws. There were no women in the Roman **Senate** and no women lawyers.

Women in a man's world

In this man's world, women had to struggle for recognition. The daughters of artists might learn the skills of the painter or sculptor. A few such as Iaia of Cyzicus (who lived about 100 BC) became successful artists.

Women who ruled as queens were thought to be dangerous. Such 'dangerous women' in the Roman world were Queen Boudicca, who led a revolt in Britain, and Cleopatra, Queen of Egypt, who bewitched two great Romans, Julius Caesar and Mark Antony, into falling in love with her. These women's public lives seemed very 'un-Roman', though each killed herself to avoid capture, an 'honourable' death in Roman eyes.

The Romans admired enemies like Zenobia, Queen of Palmyra (in Syria). This remarkable and learned queen fought off the Roman **legions** until finally being captured in AD 273. Taken to Rome, she became a Roman herself, and her daughter married the **emperor**.

A woman entertains friends by playing the *kithara*, a stringed instrument. Most women kept such skills for their private lives, at home.

A Roman woman wonders what to put next in a letter. She is writing on a wooden board, or tablet, covered with soft wax. The pen, or *stylus*, made marks in the wax. This is a wall painting from Pompeii.

Hortensia says no to taxes

A few women spoke out for their rights. Hortensia was the daughter of a famous lawyer and orator. She opposed a new tax on rich women. After the murder of Julius Caesar in 44 BC, there was civil war, and Rome's new rulers – Mark Antony, Octavian and Lepidus – needed money. They targeted more than 1400 rich Roman women. Hortensia boldly told them this was wrong. Women with no say in making laws should not be taxed to pay for a war between Romans. The politicians backed down, and agreed to tax only about 400 women. The writer Appian set down Hortensia's speech in a history of the civil wars.

The star of Roman mathematics

The most brilliant woman scientist in the Roman world was Hypatia. Her father was a professor, but she surpassed him in mathematics. Students came from all over the Roman world to study with her at Alexandria's university. Hypatia invented her own scientific instruments for her experiments. This brilliant woman met with a tragic death. On her way to classes at the university, she was seized by a fanatical mob of Christians who, calling her a magician, killed her.

Studying Roman women

Few people in history have left us as much evidence of their achievements as the Romans. **Archaeologists** have uncovered their roads, towns, **villas**, forts and temples. These discoveries reveal much about women's lives in the Roman world.

Written evidence and pictures

Most Roman writers were men, like the **historian** Tacitus who makes the occasional comment on famous women. We can read the words of a few women writers, such as the poet Sulpicia, and women scientists, such as Elephantis and Aspasia, who wrote medical and philosophy books. Unfortunately, most of the writings of Hypatia, the most famous woman mathematician of the Roman world, were lost or destroyed.

Some grafitti is by or about women. Fragments of letters and **inscriptions** on tombstones are also useful sources about Roman women's lives.

The Forum at Pompeii as it looks today. Once this large square was the business and government centre of the town. On the right stand the columns that once held up the roof of the temple of Jupiter, Pompeii's most important religious building. Pompeii is so well preserved that visitors half expect to meet a Roman strolling around the next street corner!

Pompeii – a remarkable story

Many Roman towns have been excavated by archaeologists. None is more remarkable than Pompeii, a seaside town on the Bay of Naples in Italy.

The Roman writer Pliny the Younger tells how on 24 August AD 79 the volcano Vesuvius erupted. Pompeii was buried by ash, almost 4 metres deep. It lay hidden and forgotten until people started to dig into the ruins in the 1700s. By the late 1900s much of the town had been uncovered. Houses and streets came to light once more.

The fleeing citizens had abandoned many of their possessions – furniture, silverware, work tools, kitchen pots, lamps. Many of these finds are now in museums. The town itself remains, a walkthrough 'time capsule' which allows us to recreate a vivid picture of Roman times.

Pompeii gives us a glimpse into the everyday lives of Roman women. We can see their cooking equipment, rings, hairpins and leather shoes. Most valuable of all are the wall paintings. From an age long before photography, these paintings show us the faces, the hairstyles, the jewels, and the clothes of these women who worked, raised families and helped to run a mighty **empire** almost 2000 years ago.

Women of the empire

The women of Pompeii spoke the same language (**Latin**) as other Roman women, living in countries far from Italy. Across the **empire**, men and women became 'Romanized' wherever Roman rule reached. So from an **altar** found at Westerwood on the Antonine Wall in Scotland, we learn of a woman named Vibia Pacata, possibly from Africa, whose soldier-husband Flavius Secundus came from Hungary. Two people, born in lands far apart, were together in Scotland. The world of the Roman woman was truly international.

Timeline

BC

753	Traditional date for the founding of the city of Rome
510	Romans set up a republic
264	First gladiator fights – a few women later fought in the arenas as gladiators
55	Julius Caesar lands in Britain for the first time
44	Julius Caesar is murdered

AD

43	Emperor Claudius orders army to invade Britain. Roman women begin to settle in Britain.
60	Iceni tribe, led by Queen Boudicca, revolts against Roman rule in Britain
79	Volcano Vesuvius erupts, and buries Roman towns of Pompeii, Stabiae and Herculaneum
90	Vindolanda fort in Northumberland, England is built.
101–107	Romans conquer Dacia, and the empire reaches its greatest size
c.274	Death of Zenobia, the Syrian warrior-queen, in Rome
300s	Many women in Roman Britain become Christians
370	Birth of Hypatia, the greatest woman mathematician of the Roman world
410	Last Roman soldiers leave Britain. Roman–British women are left to defend themselves.
476	Last Roman emperor in the West is overthrown by Goths. Roman Empire ends.

Sources and further reading

◄► ◄► ◄► ◄► ◄► ◄► ◄► ◄► ◄► ◄► ◄► ◄► ◄► ◄► ◄► ◄► ◄► ◄►

Sources
Daily Life in Ancient Rome,
Florence Dupont (Blackwell, 1992)
The English Heritage Book of Villas and the Roman Countryside,
Guy de la Bedoyere (English Heritage/Batsford 1993)
The Great Invasion,
Leonard Cottrell (Evans Brothers, 1958)
Greece and Rome at War,
Peter Connolly (Macdonald, 1981)
Roman Britain,
Peter Salway (Oxford University Press, 1992)
Roman Britain,
H. H. Scullard (Thames and Hudson, 1994)
The Roman Invasion of Britain,
Graham Webster (Batsford, 1993)
Roman London,
Hall and Merrifield (HMSO/Museum of London, 1986)
Roman Towns in Britain,
Guy de la Bedoyere (English Heritage/Batsford 1992)
Women in Roman Britain,
Lindsay Allason-Jones (British Museum, 1989)

Further reading
Ancient Rome,
Mike Corbishley (Facts on File/Equinox, 1989)
Family Life in Roman Britain,
Peter Chrisp (Hodder Wayland, 2001)
Look Inside a Roman Villa,
Peter Chrisp (Hodder Wayland, 2002)
Roman Villas and Great Houses,
Brenda Williams (Heinemann, 1997)
What Happened Here?: Roman Palace,
Tim Wood (A & C Black, 2000)

Glossary

altar table or other special place for making religious offerings

archaeologist expert on the past, who studies objects and evidence underground or beneath the sea

betrothal arrangement made between two families about the future marriage of a boy and girl when they grow up

cameo stone with an image such as a face carved in raised relief, used in jewellery

centurion officer roughly equivalent to a sergeant in a modern army, in charge of a century (between 80 and 100 men)

charcoal 'cooked' wood, burned as a fuel on cookers and fires

citizen Roman man who was entitled to vote in elections and serve in the legions

clan group of people, often related and sharing the same name

consul highest government official in the Roman republic; two consuls were elected each year

distaff wooden stick onto which flax or wool was wound when spinning

emperor supreme ruler of Rome; the first ruler to hold the Latin title *imperator* was Augustus

empire large area with many peoples living under rule of an emperor

festival holiday or special day, usually set aside for the worship of one god or goddess

freedwoman slave who bought or was given her freedom

frontier boundary line between one territory and another

garrison place where soldiers live, guarding a particular area

goddesses female gods

governor Roman official, often a soldier, in charge of a province

guardian adult who is responsible for bringing up a child not his or her own

henna plant used to make reddish-brown dye

historian someone who writes about past events and people

inscription writing cut into wood or stone

Latin language spoken by Romans

law codes sets of laws drawn up by the Romans

legion main battle unit of the Roman army, numbering at various times between 4000 and 6000 legionaries

linen material for clothing made from fibres of the flax plant

miscarriage when something goes wrong during pregnancy, and the unborn baby dies

mosaic decoration used on wall and floors, using small stones to make pictures and patterns

ochre kind of red clay, with iron in it

omens signs sent by the gods

orator person good at making speeches

pestle and mortar bowl and hand-held crusher used in the kitchen

pewter metal made by mixing tin and lead

provinces territories conquered and ruled by Romans, such as Britannia (Britain) and Gaul

republic form of government in early Rome, with elected officials not a king

rituals ceremonies with important religious meaning

sacrifice offering made to the gods, often of an animal newly killed

site in archaeology, place where finds about the past have been discovered, often by digging

Senate Rome's parliament, made up of important people and former officials, who advised the elected consuls

shrine place thought to be holy, where some religious object is kept

spindle weighted top-shaped piece of wood used in spinning

spinning twisting fibres together to make thread

thatched roofed with straw

tiara small crown-like head decoration, set with jewels

toga Roman garment, like a loosely folded cloak

tribe group of people sharing same beliefs, language and way of life

tripod three-legged stand for a pot or bowl

tunic long shirt-like garment

undertakers people whose job is to organize funerals

villa country farm-estate or country house

weaving making cloth or rugs by intertwining threads

widow woman whose husband has died

will instructions about what a person wants done after his or her death

Index